PONDERING GOD'S WORD

PONDERING GOD'S WORD

JEFFREY FOSTER

Seed Sowing Publications

Contents

DEDICATION

This book is dedicated to my Lord and Savior Jesus Christ, for His honor and for His glory and without whom my life would be meaningless.

To my dear wife, Lorena, for her unfailing support and encouragement in my writing journey.

To the multitude of teachers, pastors, and godly mentors that God placed in my life who played a crucial part in guiding my Christian walk, I say thank you for your diligence to serve God with compassion and steadfastness.

To you, the reader. It is my sincere desire that God would use these words to encourage you to seek a deeper understanding of His word through daily Bible reading and meditation, and that you will be inspired to be zealous in sharing the Good News of Jesus Christ.

Seed Sowing Publications
Hudson, NC USA
info@seedsowing.org

Cover Design: SelfPubBookCovers.com/RLSather

All scripture quotes are from the King James Version unless otherwise noted.

First Printing, 2023

I

Foreword

Craig and I are honored to present Jeff Foster's first book, Pondering God's Word. It is exciting to see a writer bring their work into publication and even more so when the content of that book will make a profound impact on readers for years to come. That is truly the case here.

In this book, Jeff encourages all of us to spend time in the Bible. He suggests setting time aside each day to learn more and to pray over what we read. Each chapter of the book starts with a scripture selection and ends with a prayer. Jeff has crafted his devotions carefully and has made them easy to understand. Readers will find this book a great asset for their daily devotion time.

We first met Jeff several years ago, recognized Jeff's talent as a Christian writer, and invited him to submit articles to our magazine, Faith On Every Corner. Our readers enjoy his work and look forward each month to learning more about God's Word through his writing. Jeff is dedicated to his writing craft and has a very strong and detailed style and voice. His eagerness to learn more about God's Word and wanting to share that knowledge with others is truly a blessing.

We have had the pleasure of getting to know Jeff and his wife, Lorena, over the past few years and enjoy their friendship and Christian fellowship.

Karen Ruhl, Publisher and Editor-In-Chief
Craig Ruhl, Managing Editor
Faith On Every Corner, LLC

II

Introduction

A READY VESSEL
*I could spend all my nights planning ways to serve my God
and spend all my days putting my hands to work, wearily
obtaining the praises of a few good men.
And if by grace I still attained an entrance
to God's throne room someday,
I would arrive ashamed and empty-handed.*

*Else I could spend one desperate twilight hour on my face
pleading with my Father to empty me of myself
and rest my body through the night.
Thence I would awake refreshed for the day, a ready vessel
for not mine but the Spirit's work,
casting ahead golden crowns at my Savior's feet.*

Churches today are filled with Christians who are severely lacking in devotion to God's word. I admit that I have failed many times to maintain a consistency of daily study of the Bible. But I am aware of my shortcomings, and my prayer is that God would ever increase my desire to read and meditate on His word.

The purpose of this book is to encourage the reader to set aside a quiet time each day devoted to reading and reflecting on God's word. Keep a journal and jot down a few thoughts each time you read your Bible. Write down any questions you may have; pray over those questions and ask God to help you understand what you've read. There are plenty of free online Bible commentaries and dictionaries to help you understand those unusual word definitions.

By following this simple step, I promise you that God will begin working in your life in ways that you never imagined possible.

The following pages contain a few of my own journal entries that have a special meaning to me. The longer chapters are some lessons I have taught in Bible study classes.

III

Sowing Seeds

"But he that received seed into the good ground is he that heareth the word, and understandeth it; which also beareth fruit, and bringeth forth, some an hundredfold, some sixty, some thirty". (Matthew 13:23)

As a child in the sixties almost everyone I knew had a vegetable garden. Gardens were a lot of work and Dad always assigned some chores to me. Dad always took care of the more difficult labor of clearing new plots and tilling the ground. The weeding and hoeing tasks usually fell on me. I was also called on when the harvest time came. Picking green beans, corn and tomatoes wasn't that bad, but things like squash and okra with their prickly vines and stalks always left my hands and arms itching. Although I did enjoy the fruits of our labor, garden chores were not really what a young boy wanted to do. Especially since there were nearby woods to explore, not to mention all the creatures to find and catch out of the creeks. You know an eight-year-old boy must have a pet salamander or crawdad in his pocket.

When I was a twelve, we moved across the county to a small farm and gardening chores became much more time consuming. One would think that change would strike dread in the eyes of a young boy with all the extra labor involved. But instead, I found a new attraction for the ancient vocation when I got to drive the tractor. Nothing can compare to being in control of such a powerful machine, changing the shape and texture of the earth itself. Aah, the smell of morning dew and diesel fuel. The aroma of fresh plowed earth in spring or fields of summer cut hay still stir up fond memories of a simpler time. It also reminds me of the life lessons that the never-ending hard work taught me. Painstaking preparation is essential for a life-sustaining harvest.

Jesus used the age-old knowledge of gardening and farming when he recited the parable of the sower and the seeds. He compared seeds to the word of God. We can understand that only the seeds sown in good ground, that ground which has been painstakingly prepared, can produce a bountiful harvest. Jesus gave three more scenarios in which the seed cannot produce any harvest at all. Those seeds seemingly were just wasted. But we know from the book of Isaiah, chapter fifty-five that God said His word would not return void but would accomplish His purpose and would indeed prosper.

How can we say seeds prosper if there is no harvest? Let's look again at Matthew chapter thirteen, verse four. The Bible tells us that "some seeds fell by the wayside, and the fowls came and devoured them up". The purpose of those seeds was to provide nourishment for the birds. Birds might be considered detrimental to the harvest, but they are also part of God's creation and serve their own purpose. Aren't we instructed to feed even our enemies? If we are preaching, teaching, or simply telling God's word like we're supposed to be doing then it will be spilling out to all those around us, nourishing lost souls. Just because His word may not find a lodging place in the heart of the one we are speaking to, doesn't mean it won't find a place in the mind. Who knows when some circumstance or situation will bring that word back to remembrance and finish its purpose? The Father knows.

Verses five and six tell us about the seeds that fell in stony ground and though they sprouted up they were unable to take root, so they died. Then in verse seven we read about the seeds that fell among thorns which took away all the nourishment the seeds needed to survive. With these two scenarios I believe Jesus intended to show us how we can make a difference, with His help of course.

If we want a bigger harvest on the farm that generally means we must clear some land. It means hard work. Trees need to be cut and stumps dug out. Shrubs and thorny bushes need to be cut down and rooted out. Rocks need to be broken up and carried out. The land is then plowed and harrowed to create the best environment for bringing forth and nourishing life from the seeds.

If our prayer is to enlarge God's kingdom by bringing in a greater harvest, then we need to follow the lessons Jesus taught us in His parables. Just as I was given simple tasks as a young boy in the garden, new Christians have opportunities to work and learn within the body of Christ and have a part in the benefits of an eternal harvest. Like the old farmer, with his storm weathered wiry frame, setting his mind and putting his hand to the task of expanding his fields to provide a life sustaining harvest for his ever-increasing family, the mature Christian must set his mind to expanding the reach of the gospel of Christ. A rugged expanse of deep-rooted brier bushes of sin is growing all around us, waiting to be cleared out and cultivated into fertile fields, bringing forth a bountiful harvest for our King. As the old saying goes, it takes blood, sweat, and tears to complete a job successfully. Jesus provided the blood when he sacrificed His life for ours on an old rugged cross. The Holy Spirit gives us the strength to work which will likely make us sweat. And God says that one day He will wipe away all our tears.

Remember, painstaking preparation is essential for a life-sustaining harvest.

IV

Delusion

"And for this cause God shall send them strong delusion, that they should believe a lie:" (2 Thessalonians 2:11)

Believers often associate the key verse with the radical non-believers which are so prevalent today; those that call good evil, and evil good. But in fact, Paul is warning against those in the church who have refused to accept the simplicity of God's gift of salvation. In Paul's time, the Pharisees were teaching laws which must be followed if one was to be included in God's kingdom. The problem was that God did not write those laws. They were written by the Pharisees to gain control over the people.

Much of this ideology still exists today. It is not reasonable in human terms of thinking that our salvation doesn't require us to do something to maintain it. If that were true, then the work that Jesus Christ did for us on the cross of calvary would not be perfect. If we cannot believe that Christ's work is perfect, then we lack the faith that is proof of salvation.

"That if thou shalt confess with thy mouth the Lord Jesus, and shalt believe in thine heart that God hath raised him from the dead, thou shalt be saved." (Romans 10:9)

The truth is, Jesus Christ alone has the power to forgive sin, and He asked no more from us than to trust Him in faith, turn away from our sin, and follow Him.

V

The Gospel

"Moreover, brethren, I declare unto you the gospel which I preached unto you, which also ye have received, and wherein ye stand;" (1Corinthians 15:1)

The Gospel; literally the Good News. What is this gospel that Paul speaks of? I've heard the term "gospel truth" often used to vigorously convince someone that they are not lying. It is comparing their story to a solid foundation of truth.

The gospel in the scripture reference however is the all-encompassing truth of Jesus Christ. This Gospel describes the death, burial, and resurrection of our LORD and savior. This Gospel is also the person of Jesus Christ. For us to be forgiven of our sin and be accepted into an eternal fellowship with God the Father, we must wholly believe the Gospel, the sacrificial events that took place and the person of Jesus.

We are to follow Paul's example, declaring the Gospel, so that men may receive it and be able to stand therein when Christ returns.

VI

The Beginning of Light

"And God said, Let there be light: and there was light."
(Genesis 1:3)

The Biblical account of creation is a fascinating yet mysterious subject which, because of its mystery, continues to be a target of criticism. It's not surprising that man would formulate such elaborate descriptions of how our world came into existence without any attribution to a divine being. Paul writes in 1 Corinthians 2:14, "But the natural man receiveth not the things of the Spirit of God: for they are foolishness unto him: neither can he know them, because they are spiritually discerned."
Without Christ in us we simply cannot understand the truth of God's word. We shouldn't get upset at unbelievers for claiming that our Bible is nothing more than a fairy tale. Wisdom and understanding is given to us by the Holy Spirit in His perfect timing.
Back to our key verse though, let us reflect on the creation of light. To be clear, the light in verse 3 is not the sun. God created the sun

on the fourth day.

Genesis 1:14-19 "And God said, Let there be lights in the firmament of the heaven to divide the day from the night; and let them be for signs, and for seasons, and for days, and years: And let them be for lights in the firmament of the heaven to give light upon the earth: and it was so. And God made two great lights; the greater light to rule the day, and the lesser light to rule the night: he made the stars also. And God set them in the firmament of the heaven to give light upon the earth, And to rule over the day and over the night, and to divide the light from the darkness: and God saw that it was good. And the evening and the morning were the fourth day."

So, what was this light created on the first day? A few of our Bible commentaries from the 17th and 18th century give us a bit of insight.

John Gill (1697-1771) compared the light to the pillar of fire that led the Israelites in the wilderness, in effect, Jesus Christ.

Adam Clarke (1762-1832) took a more scientific approach, giving that latent heat is present in all matter and with that heat is potential for light, (basically saying that is when God created the nature of atoms). I'm always a little leery when someone tries to use science to "prove" God's word. I think it should be the other way around.

Matthew Henry, (1662-1714), my favorite commentator but also the most difficult to understand sometimes, commits about 3 pages to elaborate on the 1st five verses. He references many verses which refer to Christ as light but also to Christ as the Word.

The first light is God manifesting His holiness and purity in a way that the crown of His creation, mankind, could understand. The entire design for God's plan for all creation was written on that 1st day. Think about it, we were loved and chosen before the foundation of the world, (Ephesians 1:4), and on the first day the earth had no foundation, it was without form and void. Jesus isn't a creation, He is from everlasting to everlasting, but the Light is Christ manifested for our understanding. The Word of the gospel was manifested in Christ on that first day.

Let's continue to verse 4, "And God saw the light, that it was good: and God divided the light from the darkness."

God saw that the light was good, but He doesn't say that about the darkness. Although the Bible doesn't tell us when angels were created, I believe the first day is when Lucifer, the angel of darkness, is separated from Christ, the Light of our salvation.

VII

God Consoles

"For I know the thoughts that I think toward you, saith the LORD, thoughts of peace, and not of evil, to give you an expected end." Jeremiah 29:11

We all make mistakes and wrong decisions in life. A wrong decision often leads us down a sinful path. Unfortunately, the bad decisions are often followed by circumstances which are difficult to endure. If we're not careful, we can let our predicament drive us into a state of depression, causing us to seemingly lose any remnant of hope. For Christians though, we have God's word that He will never leave us or forsake us. He stays by our side when we fail to acknowledge Him. God orchestrates the circumstances to guide us back on the right path if we remember to simply trust Him

Even in times of punishment God consoles His people. At the time when Jeremiah 29 was written most of Israel was held captive by the Babylonians. Some were scattered about, driven from the destroyed city of Jerusalem. Israel had refused to listen to God's pleading for them to repent from their sinful ways. Now Israel must bear the consequence of God's punishment.

In captivity, removed from their destructive sinful society, Israel finally begins to realize that they need to listen to God. He was their last hope. God was then able to show His great love and kindness to His chosen people. In verses 5-6 He begins telling them what to do in their captive environment. God tells them to build houses, plant gardens, marry and have children. In other words, be content in the situation God had placed them in and live their life. Then in Jeremiah 29:7 He continues with, "And seek the peace of the city whither I have caused you to be carried away captives, and pray unto the LORD for it: for in the peace thereof shall ye have peace."

The account in the book of Jeremiah describing Israel's fall, their punishment, and their eventual return to rebuild their home, is given to us so we can understand the nature of God's character towards His people. Those that belong to God, those that are redeemed through Christ's blood, will not be allowed to continue in sin. It is in our nature to follow distractions and temptations. But God will not allow His people to be destroyed by sin. If we stray too far out of His will into this sinful world, He will punish us in order to bring us back to Him.

"Father, thank you today for the assurance that whatever situation or circumstance we find ourselves in, Your desire is that we live with peace in our heart and mind because we do have an expected end. Amen."

VIII

Daily Battle

"In a moment, in the twinkling of an eye, at the last trump: for the trumpet shall sound, and the dead shall be raised incorruptible, and we shall be changed. For this corruptible must put on incorruption, and this mortal must put on immortality." (1Corinthians 15:52-53)

Believers awake each morning in the midst of battle. Temptations come from all directions, relentlessly trying to find our weakest point. Our natural mind struggles against our spirit, with a constant desire to succumb to temptations. We must strengthen our spirit by feeding on God's word every day, so that this corruptible mortal body will be in subjection to our immortal spirit.

"But thanks be to God, which giveth us the victory through our Lord Jesus Christ." (1Corinthians 15:57)

IX

How Long Lord?

"The LORD God is my strength, and he will make my feet like hinds' feet, and he will make me to walk upon mine high places. To the chief singer on my stringed instruments." (Habakkuk 3:19)

It doesn't take but a few minutes of watching the main-stream news media to become discouraged in our walk with Christ. Cruelty and hate are running rampant in the world. Abominable behavior is celebrated rather than despised. Society cheers on those who brazenly make a mockery of godly morals and laws. We know the Bible says, "God is not mocked". So why then does God just stand by and watch all this, seeing His children are in such distress? The deepest drawer in Lucifer's tool cabinet is labeled DISCOURAGEMENT, for that is his most reliable tool.

Habakkuk asked the same questions. "O LORD, how long shall I cry, and thou wilt not hear! even cry out unto thee of violence, and thou wilt not save!" (Habakkuk 1:2) This was during a time when

God allowed the Chaldeans to rule over Judah as a punishment for their sin. The Chaldeans were a violent people, priding themselves in the art of war, pillaging and plundering their victims. In verse 4 Habakkuk continues questioning God's reasoning, even to the point of accusing God of wrong judgment. "Therefore the law is slacked, and judgment doth never go forth: for the wicked doth compass about the righteous; therefore wrong judgment proceedeth." (Habakkuk 1:4). He simply could not understand why his prayers for relief from these evil people went seemingly unheard. Does that sound familiar? Churches are praying for the world leaders and the ungodly influence on society. Evils and immoralities continue unrestrained while the church is fervently praying against them. How long LORD must we wait?

How quickly we forget the sovereignty of God. If we're not careful we begin to put ourselves on the same level as God himself. We start believing that just because we belong to God that we have the right to judge those "terrible sinful creatures" all around us and demand our Father to strike them down.

"Behold, his soul which is lifted up is not upright in him: but the just shall live by his faith." (Habakkuk 2:4).

God reminds Habakkuk that when we think ourselves to be on a higher plane than our fellow man then we have failed to be the example to the world that God has called us to be. In verse one of this chapter Habakkuk announces that he has set himself on a tower to watch for God to protect him. However, God rebukes him for setting himself above the circumstances. When we self-righteously hide ourselves away from the evils of this world how can anyone see the strength we have from our faith? It is the confidence in our salvation and the boldness of godly living amid evil circumstances that will shine a light in the dark souls we encounter.

"O LORD, I have heard thy speech, and was afraid: O LORD, revive thy work in the midst of the years, in the midst of the years make known; in wrath remember mercy." (Habakkuk 3:2)

Habakkuk now sees that no matter what is going on around him that he will be safe in God's hands. Jesus said, "Be not afraid of them that kill the body, and after that have no more that they can do." Those who trust in Christ have a safe destination. It is our job to intercede in prayer for the salvation of those caught in the evil strongholds, not for their destruction.

"Although the fig tree shall not blossom, neither shall fruit be in the vines; the labour of the olive shall fail, and the fields shall yield no meat; the flock shall be cut off from the fold, and there shall be no herd in the stalls: Yet I will rejoice in the LORD, I will joy in the God of my salvation." (Habakkuk 3:17-18)

When we understand as Habakkuk finally did that when we seek harm to our enemies, we are failing to exhibit God's love. God sent His Son to die for ALL people because He loves ALL people unconditionally.

However difficult our struggle, whatever evil we encounter, we can rejoice because we have a sure salvation. Rejoicing makes our light brighter and perhaps, with God's grace, may draw even the vilest creature back from the precipice of the fiery pit.

"Father God, thank You for loving to me. Help me Father to make Your love known to those around me. Strengthen my faith so I may stand steadfast against the world's attempt to discourage me. In Jesus' name I ask, Amen."

X

Hungry Hearts

"And when he had sent them away, he departed into a mountain to pray." (Mark 6:46)

Jesus had spent the day teaching thousands in a desert place. The disciples still had not quite understood the significance of the miracle He had just performed before them. Five thousand men had their physical appetite satisfied with only two fish and five loaves of bread. But although Jesus had spent hours feeding the people the bread of his word, their hearts were still hungry.

In this verse Jesus sets the example for us to pray to the Father to bring forth the harvest of our ministry and satisfy the hearts and minds of men with the hope of salvation.

XI

Take Up the Staff

"And commanded them that they should take nothing for their journey, save a staff only; no scrip, no bread, no money in their purse: But be shod with sandals; and not put on two coats." (Mark 6:7-9)

There is no earthly provision necessary for us to share the gospel of Jesus Christ. As Jesus sends out the twelve apostles he instructs them, and us, what is needed to carry out His purpose in our lives. First, notice he sends them by twos. In the Old Testament law, the testimony of two witnesses was needed so that a claim could be established. The two were to encourage and help each other when unforeseen circumstances might have hindered their work. Working in pairs provided an accountability partner to keep them focused on the divine task.

Jesus gave them power. At the moment we accept Christ as our savior we receive the Holy Spirit within us, to teach us and guide our thoughts and actions according to God's will.

"a staff only" The staff is displayed throughout biblical history as an instrument of power. Men carried a staff to lean on and give support when the path was treacherous. The staff became an extension of the arm and hand to steady their way. When we lean on God all His power is applied through our hands and is available to steady our walk. What a privilege and honor it is, that the Almighty God of all the universe would enable our feeble hands with power over the unclean spirits and carry the Good News of Jesus Christ to all nations.

XII

Unbelief

"And straightway the father of the child cried out, and said with tears, Lord, I believe; help thou mine unbelief." (Mark 9:24)

How often do we pray for healing, for a change, for a miracle, then get up off our knees and, if we're honest with ourselves, truly expect to see the same circumstance as we did before we closed our eyes in prayer? Because we have limited understanding we resort to logical thinking which limits what our natural self can believe. This father desperately wanted his son to be healed, but there was no logical way that could happen. "If thou canst believe" Jesus replied. He could have simply said "trust me". Although our limited understanding prevents us from believing the illogical, we can still trust. God created our mind, and with His infinite wisdom, put limits on our understanding. He tells us that His thoughts are higher than our thoughts. He tells us to expect greater things than we ask. He tells us to humble ourselves before Him and just trust Him.

"Our Father, full of grace and mercy and love, help me today to trust You more. Father, help thou mine unbelief, that I may expect and see the miraculous works of your hands. I pray in Jesus' name, Amen."

XIII

I Go A Fishing

"Jesus saith unto them, Bring of the fish which ye have now caught." (John 21:10)

After Jesus' resurrection, his disciples weren't sure what they were supposed to be doing. Jesus wasn't walking with them every day to guide them. But Peter wasn't one to sit and wait. He had to do something. "I go a fishing" he proclaimed, and the others with him joined him on the ship. The disciples fished all night and caught nothing. These were not inexperienced fishermen. Prior to Jesus calling them to be disciples they had made their living by fishing. Thinking they would go back to their old ways since Jesus wasn't there, they found their abilities severely lacking. As the weary empty-handed disciples approached the shore, Jesus called out to them, directing the men to cast their nets on the right side of the ship. Without knowing who this man was they still obeyed His command, and the net was filled with so many fish that they couldn't pull it in and had to call for help from another boat.

God in His great mercy and kindness has given all people earthly abilities so we can work to sustain ourselves. But when we meet Jesus, and allow Him to be our master, He gives us a new occupation. When Christ first called the disciples to follow Him, He told them they would henceforth be fishers of men.

Though we still have the same abilities we had before we became Christians, now we understand that those abilities are a gift from God. We should have a desire to bring something to the table for Jesus, but without following the direction of the Holy Spirit we will always come empty handed. If we listen to His voice, Christ will work through us to fill our nets.

"Thank you, God, for giving me your Holy Spirit to live within my heart, so that I can use the abilities you have given me to bring gifts to your table. Amen"

XIV

Circle of Trust

My typical day begins at five A.M. I take a few pills which my doctor insists I need in order to stay healthy. I then sit down at my desk to enjoy my life sustaining daily bread from God's word. After a few chapters and maybe a few notes it's time to eat a light breakfast and get ready for work. My commute takes about thirty-five minutes and it is mostly two-lane roads with light traffic. During those thirty-five minutes of relative quiet I have my morning talk with my Father. My mornings have become a series of routine habits. I like having a routine. Some would say I am a "creature of habit." I am comfortable with that. It is my nature to dislike change. Any disruption of my routine tends to frustrate me. I'm no different from most people; I want to stay in my comfort zone.

A few weeks ago, on my way to work I was praying to my Father as usual. My prayers always begin with praise and gratitude. I'm specific with what I am grateful for. I think it's important to not just generalize "blessings". God blesses each of us with so much that we can't possibly name them all, but I believe it's important to name a few things that are special to us, especially if it's an answered prayer. From praise and gratitude, I move to asking forgiveness for anything I've done wrong. Next is the intercessory portion of my prayer. I had confidence in intercessory prayer because I have seen those answered many times. I have family and loved ones that I name daily to God, for protection, guidance, or comfort as the need may be. But this morning the Holy Spirit threw up a giant stop sign, freezing me in the middle of my routine.

I don't know if it was a few seconds or a few minutes, but I couldn't speak, humbled into silence by the omniscient God. Finally, the realization was prodded into my mind. I needed to pray for me first. I rarely ask anyone to pray for me. Somehow, I think it sounds selfish, especially since God has so richly blessed me with good health and provisions for life. Let me be perfectly clear though, it is NEVER selfish to ask someone to pray for you. We survive by God's grace alone and we absolutely should be praying for each other. At this particular moment, when God's Holy Spirit stopped my "routine" prayer, I realized that I needed to make some changes.

My prayer life had always included asking for help in understanding God's word, that I would glean something from it that would be a help to me in serving Him. I've asked for help in recognizing when God puts an opportunity in my path to serve in whatever capacity He chooses. I would be careful to ask that whatever is done by my hand would be seen as the work of the Holy Spirit, not by me. But the one thing that's needed that I wasn't asking for is that I would be counted as trustworthy by everyone I meet. People must trust you before they will accept anything you say or try to do for them.

We all have acquaintances, family and friends that, even though we may love them dearly, we know we can't trust them. We can't change that. What we can change however is to live our life in a manner that makes us known to be trustworthy, especially to those people that we do not trust. Although I'm sure those closest to me, those in my circle of trust, would know me as trustworthy, I realized that I was not making a conscious effort for those that I did not trust to know that. I was doing very little to make those people believe that they could safely confide in me. Without confidence in me how could anyone trust me enough to listen when I tell them about Jesus? That doesn't sound very Christ-like does it?

When Jesus walked this earth, He provided many examples of His trustworthiness. Sadly, His disciples and those close to Him were often the most forgetful of what He could accomplish for them. Nevertheless, the fame of the miracles He performed was widely known. Jesus made an intentional effort to seek out society's least desirable people of the day in order to show the power of His Father. It was an effort that caused these people, the ones that were least trusted in society, to trust Him fully. Zacchaeus, the distrusted tax collector for example, showed no hesitation when Jesus called him down out of the sycamore tree, and because he trusted Jesus, he and his family were saved. The most moving story of compassion though I believe is that of the Greek woman, a Gentile, who came begging Jesus to cast out the devil that was in her daughter. Jesus' first answer may seem cruel, but this woman knew she could fully trust Jesus to help her. Jesus was her last hope and because she was able to trust Him her daughter was healed. The compassionate, trustworthy character she saw in Jesus is the character that I need to strive for.

The Christian as an ambassador for Christ should have the same listening ear, the same helpful hand, the same compassionate heart, for the stranger as he does for the closest loved one. That is very difficult if not impossible for us to do on our own. It is simply not in our natural character. We must fully surrender to Christ and allow Him to change our character. Our character should, without any trace of doubt, show us trustworthy to whoever we meet, whether it be a hated tax collector or an outcast foreigner.

And now I humbly ask you to pray for me, that I would be considered trustworthy to anyone that crosses my path, so that I might be trusted to point someone to Jesus, whether a trusted loved one or an unknown stranger.

"For a certain woman, whose young daughter had an unclean spirit, heard of him, and came and fell at his feet: The woman was a Greek, a Syrophenician by nation; and she besought him that he would cast forth the devil out of her daughter. But Jesus said unto her, Let the children first be filled: for it is not meet to take the children's bread, and to cast it unto the dogs. And she answered and said unto him, Yes, Lord: yet the dogs under the table eat of the children's crumbs. And he said unto her, For this saying go thy way; the devil is gone out of thy daughter. And when she was come to her house, she found the devil gone out, and her daughter laid upon the bed." (Mark 7:25-30)

XV

Train Up a Child

"And whosoever shall offend one of these little ones that believe in me, it is better for him that a millstone were hanged about his neck, and he were cast into the sea." (Mark 9:42)

This verse often brings to mind the instructions from the Old Testament book of wisdom, Proverbs 22:6, "Train up a child in the way he should go: and when he is old, he will not depart from it." But in verse 42, Jesus is using the example of a child to show John's wrongdoing when he stated in verse 38, "Master, we saw one casting out devils in thy name, and he followeth not us: and we forbad him, because he followeth not us."

The man casting out demons was a child in Christ, simply doing all he knew to do to further the kingdom of God. We must be careful not to hinder the work of the Holy Spirit in those babes in Christ. Train up a child...train up a new believer, each has the same effect. When they are mature, they shall not depart from God.

XVI

⁘

Honoring God Through Adversity

I think we all understand what adversity is after what we have seen in the world during the 2020 pandemic. We have either lived it or felt it through someone we love. Adversities can either make us get serious about our prayer life or drive us further away from God depending on our attitude. We all go through trials sometime in our life. Some folks it seems have much more than others. But we can be assured that God is able to use each trial we go through to increase our faith and ultimately bring glory to His son, Jesus.

"Why do we even have these trials?" you may ask. Adversity comes about in our life from three different sources.

Firstly, God sometimes creates a trial to test our faith, such as when He commanded Abraham to sacrifice his son Isaac. I can't imagine placing any child on an altar to take its life as a willing sacrifice. Thankfully, God does not put trials on us greater than we are able to bear without providing a means of escape. God provided a substitute sacrifice for Abraham, a way to escape this trial, because he was obedient to God's command. And because of Abraham's faith and obedience during this trial, we are still blessed today.

> Genesis 22:17-18 "That in blessing I will bless thee, and in multiplying I will multiply thy seed as the stars of the heaven, and as the sand which is upon the sea shore; and thy seed shall possess the gate of his enemies; And in thy seed shall all the nations of the earth be blessed; because thou hast obeyed my voice."

"all the nations of the earth" That's us today. When we get to heaven we need to tell Abraham how grateful we are that he was obedient in that trial.

Secondly, adversities can come our way from attacks by someone else or even Satan himself, through no fault of our own. Job is a well known example of this type of adversity. Poor old Job probably never knew while he was here on earth what caused his horrible trial. He also didn't know that his story would be told for thousands of years to come. How often have we been comforted by Job's story when we face things we don't understand? Through his story we can see the sovereignty of God. He reminds us that God is not taken by surprise by the circumstances that so easily upset us. God is fully in control of the situation and already has a plan for how He will use it to strengthen our faith, if we simply stay steadfast in our obedience to Him.

The third way that adversities attack us is where I think we see God's great mercy and grace most clearly. Sometimes we just bring on the adversities ourselves. We know that disobedience or rebellion will get us in trouble. But some-times, we get a little to comfortable with our abilities and start making decisions, big and small, without seeking guidance from the Holy Spirit. We may be okay for a while, but eventually we'll make a wrong decision that gets us in trouble. Thankfully, God knew before the foundation of the world about our times of rebellion, our times of disobedience, our times of simply ignoring His divine guidance. Therefore, He made a plan to bring us through those times of self-inflicted adversities and make something beautiful out of the messes we make. The story of Jonah is an example of God using a rebellious and disobedient servant to show His power over the sea and a big fish. Even with Jonah's bad attitude God still used him to bring a wicked city to repentance.

Adverse circumstances can sometimes make us want to throw up our hands and quit. If we allow them, struggles and trials can move us away from God. Many times, when problems arise our instinct is to try to fix them. As Christians though, we know that we need to allow God to fix our problems. But then our sinful nature comes out again, and we tend to try to figure out how a problem should be fixed and then we pray for God to fix it our way. Anyone else besides me guilty on that one? That doesn't ever really work out does it? The problem with that way of thinking is that when we can't see any way to fix a problem then we don't bother asking God because we don't know how to tell Him how to fix it. That puts us in dangerous territory. Even if we do continue praying, we aren't surrendering our all to Him and any prayer is hindered because we aren't dealing with the trial. I know from painful experience that God will let us just wallow there until we're ready to surrender the problem to Him and trust Him to do whatever He wants to with it. When we do finally surrender, God first works on our heart to root out our rebellious and prideful nature. Then He might change our circumstances, or more likely He makes us realize that we are safe with Him no matter what trial we are in. The size of our adversity is insignificant compared to the size of our God.

Christine Gorman, a noted medical science writer said this in an article in Time Magazine, in the July 28, 2003 edition;

"Perhaps because their brains are wired differently, dyslexics are often skilled problem solvers, coming at solutions from novel or surprising angles and making conceptual leaps. ... It may also be that their early struggle with reading better prepares them for dealing with adversity in a volatile, fast-changing world."

Just as the dyslexic's analytic skills are strengthened through his early struggles, the Christian's faith is strengthened through adversities. God prepares us for the greater trials by teaching us to look to Him in the smaller problems. Can you name one biblical character that did not go through some sort of trial or adversity?

God uses His Word to prepare us for each day and for what lies ahead. The Bible if full of examples of people serving God through various trials. God simply calls us to obedience. Nowhere did God say do this but wait until it's safer or do this but wait until they stop the persecution or do this but wait for a more convenient time.

Did God tell Moses to go bring His people out of Egypt, but wait and watch for Pharaoh to be in a good mood? No, of course not. When God gives a commandment He means now, no matter what we must face to accomplish it.

There are many important reasons to stay steadfast in honoring God through an adversity but let us focus on the three primary ones based on different biblical scenarios.

First, faithfulness during an adversity prepares us for what lies ahead. In Daniel, chapter 6 we find the familiar story of Daniel and the lion's den. Daniel was held captive in Babylon. He no longer had the freedom he enjoyed in Israel. He, no doubt was in adverse circumstances, through no fault of his own. But Daniel never gave up what God had called him to do. He still prayed three times per day just as he did before he was taken prisoner, and he made no secret of it. God blessed him for his faithfulness by moving him to the highest position in Babylon, just below the king. That didn't sit too well with the Babylonian princes and governors who were under his authority. They conspired together to trick king Darius into signing a decree which would certainly have Daniel sentenced to death for simply continuing in his faith.

> "Now when Daniel knew that the writing was signed, he went into his house; and his windows being open in his chamber toward Jerusalem, he kneeled upon his knees three times a day, and prayed, and gave thanks before his God, as he did aforetime." (Daniel 6:10)

Continuing to serve through adverse or even dangerous circumstances requires us to spend more time in prayer and meditation in God's word. We need to allow our Father to draw us in to a closer relationship with our Him. That's where we find peace and contentment that only He can give us, and the greater level of faith we need to be a steadfast servant in times of trials. That greater faith gave Daniel the boldness to remain steadfast even in the face of almost certain death. God rewarded Daniel's steadfast faith by keeping the lion's mouths closed that night. Being steadfast not only kept him safe that night, but God also used Daniel's faithfulness to turn the heart of King Darius.

> "Then king Darius wrote unto all people, nations, and languages, that dwell in all the earth; Peace be multiplied unto you. I make a decree, That in every dominion of my kingdom men tremble and fear before the God of Daniel: for he is the living God, and steadfast for ever, and his kingdom that which shall not be destroyed, and his dominion shall be even unto the end. He delivereth and rescueth, and he worketh signs and wonders in heaven and in earth, who hath delivered Daniel from the power of the lions."
> (Daniel 6:25-27)

Secondly, faithfulness during the trial gives confidence to other Christians around us. Simply put, we need each other. We need God to watch over us, we need Jesus to save us, we need the Holy Spirit to guide and comfort us, but we also need our church body to encourage and build us up. God's word tells us in 1 Thessalonians 5:11 "Wherefore comfort yourselves together, and edify one another, even as also ye do." What better way is there to encourage one another than by being a steadfast example of faith during our adversities?

Paul wrote in Philippians 1:13-14 "So that my bonds in Christ are manifest in all the palace, and in all other places; And many of the brethren in the Lord, waxing confident by my bonds, are much more bold to speak the word without fear." The ASV translation says it this way; "more abundantly bold—fearlessly to speak the word"

Paul was in prison when he wrote this, preaching to whomever he encountered. He was writing letters to the churches he started, to give them encouragement, instruction, and sometimes admonishment. Wherever he is, he strives to be a godly example to those that look to him for guidance.

One example that I can look back on was a Sunday School teacher I had years ago. He made a powerful impact on me by his faithfulness during a difficult time. His infant grandson had passed away unexpectedly, and the funeral was on a Saturday afternoon. It was certainly a heart-breaking circumstance for him and his daughter. He would not have been questioned by anyone in the class if had asked someone to fill in and teach for him the next morning. But no, he was there, and delivered a well-prepared lesson as always. My respect for him was greatly multi-plied that day. I was challenged that day to strive for a higher level of steadfastness in my own faith.

Thirdly, and this one is the most critical reason to honor God during the adversity, faithfulness during the trial will manifest our unwavering trust in the sovereignty of God to unbelievers, so that they may know that He is the LORD.

> "Again in the ninth year, in the tenth month, in the tenth day of the month, the word of the LORD came unto me, saying, Son of man, write thee the name of the day, even of this same day: the king of Babylon set himself against Jerusalem this same day." (Ezekiel 24:1-2)

God set up King Nebuchadnezzar to put Jerusalem under siege as a punishment for their rebellion against Him. In verse three, He begins the parable of the boiling pot to de-scribe the state of Jerusalem and the impending judgment they were about to receive for their rebellion against God. At one point He compares them to the bloody scum that rises to the top of the boiling pot of meat that was not properly cleaned. The pot is then emptied of the good meat and set back in the fire to burn off the filthy scum, a way of cleansing the pot. The pot here represents the city of Jerusalem, and the improperly prepared meat is the rebellious and sinful people.

As God prepares Ezekiel to deliver His message, He also puts him in a trial as well. The key verse in this chapter here though is verse 16 - "Son of man, lo, I am taking from thee the desire of thine eyes by a stroke, and thou dost not mourn, nor weep, nor let thy tear come." (Ezekiel 24:16)

You may have lost a spouse or someone very dear to you and know firsthand how difficult it would have been for Ezekiel to keep his emotions hidden. Ezekiel was to be an example to the people by showing his trust in God's wisdom and sovereignty, no matter the circumstance.

I think we may be seeing the beginnings of God's judgment for the horrible sins in this world. We should never act surprised or sorrowful over God's judgment. It's a part of who God is. To Christians, when we see a nation or people defying God, it is our job to give the warning, intercede in prayer for their salvation, and show ourselves to be content and trusting in God's sovereignty. People take notice of that.

"Thus Ezekiel is unto you a sign: according to all that he hath done shall ye do: and when this cometh, ye shall know that I am the Lord GOD. Also, thou son of man, shall it not be in the day when I take from them their strength, the joy of their glory, the desire of their eyes, and that whereupon they set their minds, their sons and their daughters, That he that escapeth in that day shall come unto thee, to cause thee to hear it with thine ears? In that day shall thy mouth be opened to him which is escaped, and thou shalt speak, and be no more dumb: and thou shalt be a sign unto them; and they shall know that I am the LORD."
(Ezekiel 24:24-27)

If we are always complaining about our circumstances or what is going on in the world then we can't be a believable witness for Christ. Our job is to manifest the hope we have in Christ, to let our light shine. We make Christ attractive to those around us by staying steadfast in our faith during the adversities and trials that most people would find hopeless. When we commit ourselves to honor God, He will use us to bring hope to a lost and dying world.

"Let your light so shine before men, that they may see your good works, and glorify your Father which is in heaven."
(Matthew 5:16)

XVII

Can You See?

"They that go down to the sea in ships, that do business in great waters; These see the works of the LORD, and his wonders in the deep". (Psalm 107:23-24)

They that go....see.

The seafaring crew are gifted to observe how mighty is the power of God. He raises up terrible storms with his hand. He brings stillness and peace in the midst of the treacherous crashing wave with just a simple word.

Only the soldier on the front-lines of battle can truly understand the horrors of warfare. He learns firsthand the cost of victory is paid through excruciating pain and bloodshed, untold sacrifices, and even life itself.

Those who linger back, those who allow their fear to nullify their hunger, will never understand the cost of victory. They may cheer and sing of victory, they may enjoy the benefits, but can never fully appreciate the spoils of battle.

The Bible tells us that many are called but few are chosen. The man who overcomes his fear with faith will see the mighty works of God firsthand. He will experience the power of God working in hearts and lives of a suffering and needy people. He will watch as that sailor did, as God bring stillness out of the dreadful storm.

Blessed is the man who in humble faith answers God's call to go.

XVIII

Looking Forward to
Our Rest

"There remaineth therefore a rest to the people of God."
Hebrews 4:9

Webster's defines rest in several ways. A few of them are freedom from activity or labor. peace of mind or spirit, to be free from anxiety or disturbance, and also a rhythmic silence in music.
We can see examples of all these definitions in God's Word. God rested on the seventh day after His six days of work of creation, (ref. Genesis 2:2). We can have peace of mind and be free from anxiety when we "Rest in the LORD, and wait patiently for him", (Psalm 37:7a). Jesus is resting at the right hand of the His Father, a brief rhythmic quiet intermission between His finished work on the cross and His triumphant return to claim His church bride and destroy the enemy, (ref. Psalm 110:1).
But for us, those who are the people of God, we have a rest that

"remaineth", one to look forward to. How do get to that rest? A work must be done, energy must be exhausted in order for a rest to be applicable. It cannot be called rest if no work has been done beforehand.

What is this work? Jesus said "Go ye therefore, and teach all nations, baptizing them in the name of the Father, and of the Son, and of the Holy Ghost:" (Matthew 28:19). All nations mean all countries around the globe, but it also includes our next-door neighbor, our family members, our co-workers, and classmates. Nations are made up of people. All nations mean ALL people.

How long must we work before we reach our rest? Jesus also said, "And the gospel must first be published among all nations." (Mark 13:10). Man's life is but a vapor, that appears for a little time, and then vanishes away. We must work tirelessly to publish the gospel to all people while we still have breath. Only then will our work be complete, and we may enter in to our rest.

"Gracious Father, thank you for the promise of rest when my work is complete. Give me strength for the day for the tasks You have placed before me. In Jesus' name I humbly pray. Amen."

XIX

Fasting Labs

I had "fasting labs" last week. Doc's words, not mine. In my words it's having to wait for breakfast four hours past my normal eating time so they can gouge a needle in my arm while my stomach is growling so they can get a few vials of blood. I guess they think the word "fasting" won't scare me because after all, it's a biblical thing. But I see through their little game.

Intermittent fasting diet. Another misleading phrase. Somehow using an old biblical word in a new fad diet is supposed to make it appealing? I don't think so. Starving for a day or two to make the temptation of gluttony even greater. No thank you.

Seriously though, true biblical fasting however when done according to God's instructions can produce astounding results. What is fasting? How does it benefit me? Reasonable questions. But if we begin fasting with only expectations of benefiting ourselves then we need not bother. Israel learned some hard lessons when they began to question why God wasn't blessing them for their times of fasting. In Isaiah 58 verse 3 they ask "Wherefore have we fasted, say they, and thou seest not? wherefore have we afflicted our soul, and thou takest no knowledge?" But God was quick to answer in verse 4, "Behold, ye fast for strife and debate, and to smite with the fist of wickedness: ye shall not fast as ye do this day, to make your voice to be heard on high."

Fasting requires a humble heart. A humble heart does not seek its own benefit but is searching out the true will of God, asking Him to intervene in a situation to bring glory to God, but being fully content with whatever He does. King David fasted and begged God for seven days to let his sick child live. But when the child died on the seventh day he got up, washed, put on clean clothes and went into the house of the LORD and worshiped. When asked about his actions he answered in 2 Samuel 12:22-23 "And he said, While the child was yet alive, I fasted and wept: for I said, Who can tell whether GOD will be gracious to me, that the child may live? But now he is dead, wherefore should I fast? can I bring him back again? I shall go to him, but he shall not return to me." He accepted God's will and in the process his faith was stronger, and God blessed him with another son, Solomon.

Is there a difference in Old Testament and New Testament fasting? Let's compare the instructions from Isaiah chapter 58 to that from Jesus in Matthew chapter 6.

Isaiah 58:6-7 says, "Is not this the fast that I have chosen: to loose the bonds of wickedness, to undo the bands of the yoke, and to let the oppressed go free, and that ye break every yoke? (7) Is it not to deal thy bread to the hungry, and that thou bring the poor that are cast out to thy house? when thou seest thee naked, that thou cover him; and that thou hide not thyself from thine own flesh?"

In other words, do not take advantage of the poor and weak but instead take the food you are giving up in fasting and give it to the hungry. Give shelter to the homeless and clothes to those in need. Do not limit your generosity to loved ones close to you but consider all men the same as you are with the same needs.

Compare that to what Jesus said in Matthew 6:16-18; "Moreover when ye fast, be not, as the hypocrites, of a sad countenance: for they disfigure their faces, that they may appear unto men to fast. Verily I say unto you, They have their reward. But thou, when thou fastest, anoint thine head, and wash thy face; That thou appear not unto men to fast, but unto thy Father which is in secret: and thy Father, which seeth in secret, shall reward thee openly."

Basically "be not weary in well-doing." Fasting is encouraged, but it is not an excuse to neglect our daily responsibilities or making a show of our fasting by putting on a sad face. That does nothing to bring glory to God but instead focuses attention on ourselves. Fasting is a private matter between you and God. By giving up something we need, (or think we need) in order to seek God's face we are saying to God that we are wholly relying on Him and we are serious about our need for His answer to our prayer. It is saying I trust you God to sustain me. It is saying that whatever answer He gives is sufficient.

I can attest to the fact that prayer with fasting will bring you closer to God and you will see results if done according to God's word. It doesn't need to be difficult. Set a time limit, seven days or even forty days. Give something up that you think is a necessity. It could be something as simple as your morning coffee. Spend the extra time praying and meditating over God's word. Be specific with your prayer. Call out the name of that loved one who hasn't surrendered to Christ. Call out that circumstance, that sickness, that mountain that seems impossible to cross over. Most importantly, pray believing that God will hear and answer. I promise you that God will give you a reason to praise Him.

XX

Memories

When I first met my wife back in the years BC., (before cellphones), she had an amazing talent of remembering the phone number of everyone she knew. That gift has long faded away as there is no longer a need. Now we can quickly recall the numbers of thousands of contacts in a little handheld device that is always within reach. The online version of Psychology Today magazine has a very detailed definition of memory with lots of fancy medical terms if you're interested in that sort of thing. If you want the plain English version just stick with me here. Basically, there are two types of memory, things we've experienced and things we've learned. It's best to have a good balance of both types.

We rely on our memory to tell stories from our past experiences. Some stories are used to teach a lesson, but some are purely for our nostalgic entertainment. When I was growing up we had annual family reunions, usually in September. There was always plenty of good food and we always ate more than we should. After we ate we'd gather in small groups under the shade trees with our folding chairs and the older folks would begin spinning their tales of a time gone by. We had heard most of the stories before but from year to year the details would change a little as memories faded further in the past.

We all have stories from our memory that others can learn from. The best teachers combine experience memories with learned memories in order to paint an illustration of the subject that is being taught. When we as Christians share the gospel message of Jesus Christ, we do exactly that. We combine our salvation experience and what God has done in our lives with what we have learned from studying God's word to tell a story that will hopefully lead them to follow Jesus. The word that frightens so many Christians, "witnessing", is simply telling a story drawn from our memory of what Jesus has done for us and why we chose to follow Him.

God ordained many methods to help us remember things that are important. He understands that we sometimes have trouble remembering. The great commentator Matthew Henry wrote this when explaining the fourth chapter of the book of Joshua, "But God, knowing their frame, and how apt they had been soon to forget his works, ordered an expedient for the keeping of this in remembrance to all generations, that those who could not, or would not, read the record of it in the sacred history, might come to the knowledge of it by the monument set up in remembrance of it,"

The Lord commanded Joshua to build a stone monument as a reminder of when He held back the waters of the Jordan River so the children of Israel could pass into their promised land, because He knew they would soon forget. God set the rainbow in the sky to remind us He would never again destroy the world with a flood. The greatest reminder of all though is His word that we can read every day in the Bible.

Everyone has their own unique memories. Some are pleasant such as those nostalgic memories of family reunions. Some can be bittersweet when we think of loved ones that have passed on. Some memories can cause anxieties and fear when we think about tragic events or circumstances from our past. All of our memories wrapped up together are a part of who we are and show how God has worked in our life. God uses our memory to show us that He has sovereign control over each event in our life. When we are distressed, He sometimes gives us virtual "monuments" to remind us we can find comfort in Him. When I hear that old hymn, The Old Rugged Cross, it's a reminder to me of our church congregation singing on a Sunday night in 1971 when I trusted Jesus as my Savior. Thank God for memories.

"I will remember the works of the LORD: surely I will remember thy wonders of old." (Psalms 77:11)

XXI

Be Careful What You
Ask For

"And looking up to heaven, he sighed, and saith unto him, Ephphatha, that is, Be opened. And straightway his ears were opened, and the string of his tongue was loosed, and he spake plain." (Mark 7:34-35)

Jesus sighed. The sigh was in no way an indication that the miracle He was about to perform was a difficulty or nuisance as our sighs sometimes signify. No, this sigh was one of sympathy, perhaps even pity. This deaf and dumb man's greatest desire was to be rid of his disability that set him apart from everyone else. Jesus knew that by granting this man's desire, he would also be burdened with greater responsibilities and temptations. In James chapter three we are warned of the destructive power of an untamed tongue.

By nature, we always seek the greater gift. It is difficult without the help of the Holy Spirit to be content with what we have. Jesus teaches, "For unto whomsoever much is given, of him shall be much required". There will always be temptations to use our abilities for temporary earthly gain. However, we are granted gifts from God so that we can make eternal gains for His kingdom.

"Father, this morning I pray that you would guard my thoughts...guard my tongue. Help me lay aside the temptation to use what you have given me for my own selfish gain. Make clear the path to serve you today. In Jesus' name I ask, Amen."

XXII

When the Path Isn't Clear

"Therefore leaving the principles of the doctrine of Christ, let us go on unto perfection; not laying again the foundation of repentance from dead works, and of faith toward God, Of the doctrine of baptisms, and of laying on of hands, and of resurrection of the dead, and of eternal judgment. And this will we do, if God permit." Hebrews 6:1-3

Every young child while visiting with aunts or uncles or other extended family is inevitably asked the question which he probably doesn't have a clue as to the real answer. What do you want to be when you grow up? I had my definitive answer sometime around the year 1970. I was going to be a fighter pilot in the US Air Force. Now that decision may have been influenced by the odor of Testor's plastic model glue while assembling my 1/64th scale model of the F14 Tomcat. I spent many hours in the library reading all I could find about my newly chosen career. But alas all my plans were soon dashed to pieces when I read that one of the requirements for fighter pilots was having 20/20 vision. And so it was that my half blind right eye crushed my dreams and pushed me back into the same position as the rest of the nine year old kids I knew; not a clue.

Eventually I did settle into a career path, one that I have enjoyed for the most part. Being a bit rebellious in my younger days while choosing the starting point of my path I encountered many twists and turns which probably made the journey more difficult than it needed to be. "Learn by doing" was my philosophy. With each step of the way I learned new things and found ways to use what I had learned from my experiences to boldly accept and conquer new challenges. The difficult experiences quickly gave me opportunities to lead and teach those coming up behind me. While leading and teaching presents its own set of challenges it also provides the most satisfaction.

Our Christian journey, like our career path, can take many unexpected turns and run into difficulties. Those turns and difficulties, and the times we just don't know which way to go, can stagnate us. We think God isn't speaking or giving us direction so we just sit down and wait. At the end of the day how much reward, how much fruit, will be there if we just wait? Nothing. On our workplace job we are usually expected to keep doing what we are told until we are told to do something different. We can't expect to clock in each morning and expect someone to come retrain us for some unknown task. Our Christian path is no different. "Learn by doing" should be the way of life for every Christian.

In chapter 6 of Hebrews the writer tells us to leave the principles of the doctrine of Christ and go on to perfection. That doesn't mean abandon or turn from the doctrine of the gospel of Christ. It means we have all we need to serve Christ the moment we receive Him as our Lord and Savior. We cannot sit down to learn all we need before we put our hand to the task. The word perfection in verse 1 means equipped for duty. We are given that perfection the day the Holy

Spirit takes up residence within us. We still need a quiet time each day to read and meditate on God's Word but waiting cannot be an option. Time is short and the fields are white unto harvest.

Learn by doing. "And this will we do, if God permit."

XXIII

Treasures

As I get older I have less and less attraction for material possessions. Oh yes, there was a time that I sought after the faster cars, the finer house, antiquities with their decorative novelty, and whatever else might catch a young man's eye. But there came a time when those things required just too much time and energy to maintain, not to mention space to display or store them. Maybe I just realized that none of those things really matter on the eternal scale.

There are some treasures though that we want to hang on to for some sentimental reason, ones that stir up memories of hopes and dreams of a time gone by. One of my elementary school classmate friends is struggling through the burdensome task of cleaning out her parents house, the house she grew up in, to prepare to put it on the market. Both of her parents are in nursing care and with their declining health she knows they will never need that old house again. She made an interesting discovery while going through the various objects in the home. Her mother had written notes, some with markers directly on the object, and some with paper notes taped to the objects, describing in just a few words where they came from and what made them memorable. What foresight this dear mother had in making sure the precious memories she had would someday be passed along to her children so that maybe they would last just a little while longer.

There are a few things however that have come into my possession that I will cherish until the day that I leave this world. On the last Sunday in July of 2005 I taught my first Sunday School class lesson. The title of the lesson was "What is Hope?" and the scripture text was from Ezekiel chapter 43. Still today I tend to shy away from public speaking and I'm sure that day I was a basket case of nerves. But that afternoon whatever fears I had of knowing whether or not I was serving in God's will were completely and utterly wiped away. That Sunday afternoon we stopped in to visit my aunt, my dad's youngest sister. I had not told her that I was teaching that morning for the first time and had not yet mentioned it when she told me she had something to give me. What she placed in my hands drove solidly home the lesson I taught just a few hours before. A little black Soul Winner's New Testament. I had received one of the little red Gideon Testaments before then, but what made this one special was when I opened it to the presentation page. On that page, I saw my name written in a familiar handwriting style I will never forget, that of my Pa-Pa. He had intended to give me this Testament on February 5th, 1974, thirty-one years earlier. I don't know what happened that he was unable to give it to me then but I'm claiming that it was God's perfect timing. Pa-Pa passed suddenly in 1977, just a few weeks after my fifteenth birthday. He was a man that showed unconditional love to all his grandchildren. He was a fair and honest man but sadly I don't remember him ever going to church or saying anything that would give an indication of faith. I do remember the story of a couple men coming to invite my Pa-Pa to come to church. He gave them the same excuse that I've heard when I've witnessed to people and I'm sure many of you have, "I wouldn't fit in with church people. I can't give up my drinking." And the answer they gave him still breaks my heart when I think about it. They told him that it was okay, they liked to drink a little too. Pa-Pa told them if that's the kind of hypocritical church men they were that he wanted no part of it and promptly ran them out of his yard. Sad story, yes, but when my aunt placed that little book in my hand, on that particular day, and I read who scribbled my name on the presentation page, a hope gushed forth in me that could only come from my heavenly Father. Maybe my Pa-Pa had trusted Jesus, and he certainly wanted me to. Jesus' words recorded in Matthew chapter seven said this, "Even so every good tree bringeth forth good fruit; but a corrupt tree bringeth forth evil fruit." This treasure, this little black Soul Winner's Testament with my name written on the first page, was my Pa-Pa's "good fruit". In this treasure I have hope.

Jesus taught in Matthew chapter 6, verses 19-21 that the treasures we collect on earth are only temporary, that decay would one day take them from us. He taught that we should use our efforts to lay up for ourselves treasures in heaven. We can do that by living our life in surrendered obedience to God. Earthly treasures, those material things we want to hold on to, can stir up a sense of ungodly pride if we're not careful.

God does however ordain or allow earthly treasures to accomplish His divine plan and to provide peace and hope within the hearts of His children. The Ark of the Covenant for instance, taught Israel to reverence God by representing His presence in their midst. It was still a temporary treasure, crafted by man's hands according to God's direction. God instructed Joshua to set up the twelve stones to be a reminder to future generations of how He heaped up the waters of the overflowing Jordan river to provide a safe passageway into the promised land. And I believe, God's watchful eye and caring hands were on a tiny sprout which would one day grow into a towering tree to be cut down and used to make the paper on which a treasured pocket-sized soul winner's Testament would be printed; because He loved a filthy, wretched sinner like me so much that He wanted to give me assurance that I was in His will at that particular moment on that last Sunday afternoon in July of 2005.

The greatest treasure that we can possess here on earth however is not something made with hands. We cannot touch it, we cannot see it, but it provides a comfort and assurance that all the treasures of the world could never provide. That is the treasure of salvation, a gift from God, by His grace, through faith in Jesus Christ. I think Paul said it best in his second letter to the church in Corinth.

"But we have this treasure in earthen vessels, that the excellency of the power may be of God, and not of us." (2 Corinthians 4:7)

Therefore, take comfort in God's boundless supply of the treasure of His grace through His Son, Jesus Christ.

XXIV

Herod's Guilt

"But when Herod heard thereof, he said, It is John, whom
I beheaded: he is risen from the dead."
(Mark 6:16)

As the fame of Jesus' ministry begin to spread, so did the rumors.
I think it's interesting that the people speculated that Jesus was a
prophet risen from the dead rather than believe the scripture's fore-
telling of the promised Messiah. Some believed He was Elijah or one
of the other Old Testament prophets. But the recently slain John
the Baptist was fresh in Herod's memory.

Herod's belief stemmed from the guilt of killing an innocent man
of God. He had respected John the Baptist. Herod had listened to
John's preaching many times and protected him as a matter of his
respect. But Herod fell into sinful lust and married a forbidden
woman, the wife of his brother. John warned Herod of the consequences of his wrong-doing which angered the king to the point
of sending him to prison. The ill-gotten wife later coerced the king

into beheading John the Baptist.

We have no record of Herod repenting or becoming a follower of Christ, but we can find a relevant lesson from his life. When we disregard a portion of God's word because of some sin we want to hold on to, we drive a wedge into our relationship with Christ. The Bible is like a mirror that allows us to see ourselves through God's eyes. Perhaps you have a corner of your mirror covered up thinking God can't see it if you keep it hidden. But the Father sees all.

Allow yourself to see all of you, lay it out before God, and experience His faithfulness, His grace, His mercy, and His love.

XXV

Why Do Bad Things
Happen to Good People

Why do bad things happen to good people? I bet you've heard that question countless times like I have. The short answer is sin. The Bible tells us that the wages of sin is death. The sinful nature of our flesh brings on all manner of trials, disease, pain, and eventually death of the body.

There is a higher purpose however for the sufferings that Christians endure. Followers of Christ have the Holy Spirit dwelling in them. Jesus told His disciples that when He went away, He would send a Comforter to teach and guide them. The Comforter, also called the Holy Spirit, enables us to endure and thrive even during the worst circumstances that we may suffer. We become intimately familiar with the peace of God that is beyond all understanding.

Still, why must I go through this pain? I can love and serve God just as much without the sufferings, can't I?

Paul teaches us in his second letter to the Corinthian church that we must suffer and be comforted so that we can understand how to give comfort to others. By offering comfort to the suffering, we can show the hope and peace we have in us from our Comforter. Our compassion can spark a desire in others to call on the Savior, asking Jesus to trade their heavy burden for His lighter burden, and receive the Comforter within themselves.

"For as the sufferings of Christ abound in us, so our consolation also aboundeth by Christ. And whether we be afflicted, it is for your consolation and salvation, which is effectual in the enduring of the same sufferings which we also suffer: or whether we be comforted, it is for your consolation and salvation." (2 Corinthians 1:5-6)

XXVI

The Consecrated Tongue

"What? know ye not that your body is the temple of the Holy Ghost which is in you, which ye have of God, and ye are not your own? For ye are bought with a price: therefore glorify God in your body, and in your spirit, which are God's." (1 Corinthians 6:19-20)

What does the word "consecrated" mean? Webster's defines it this way; "to declare to be sacred or holy : set apart for a sacred purpose". When God saves us, He declares us sacred and holy for His purposes. We are chosen to be His *peculiar people*. (1 Peter 2:9) When we accept Christ as the Savior of our soul our physical body also belongs to Him. Jesus paid the price for us with His blood on the cross. Just as the church is the body of Christ and each member of the church body is consecrated to specific services for Christ, so should each member of our individual bodies be consecrated to the work of the Holy Spirit which lives within us. Over the next five chapters we will look at different parts of our body and see what

God says about their specific use.

James had much to say about the importance of controlling our tongue in. In chapter three he compares the tongue to a horse's bit and a ship's rudder, each relatively small parts but when kept under vigilant care are able to turn about the whole body or ship. Likewise, when the tongue is carefully guarded and directed by the power of the Holy Spirit it is capable of comforting, encouraging, enlightening, and convincing lost souls to surrender to Christ. James also compares the tongue to a little fire, which when under control gives warmth and comfort. However, if left unencumbered to our sinful nature the tongue will kindle a fire that affects the course of nature and way of life for generations to come, fueled only by the forces of hell.

> "Whoso keepeth his mouth and his tongue keepeth his soul from troubles." (Proverbs 21:23)

The Christian does well in keeping or guarding his words. Our natural tendency is to speak as quickly as we think. We know that seldom works to our advantage. Our thoughts need to be weighed out, carefully meditated upon, scrutinized to make sure they align with God's word. Even then we should take counsel of the Holy Spirit to know if our thoughts when turned into words will bring honor to God. Our quietness often brings more honor than volumes of our words. Therefore our daily prayer should be as Psalms 141:3; "Set a watch, O LORD, before my mouth; keep the door of my lips."

> "A wholesome tongue is a tree of life: but perverseness therein is a breach in the spirit." (Proverbs 15:4)

A wholesome tongue is one that edifies and benefits the hearer. The word wholesome here means healing. The speech of a wholesome or healing tongue gives truths and pardons. It gives instruction and counsel in the gospel message of Jesus Christ, the path of righteousness to the tree of life whose leaves are for the healing of all nations. A perverse tongue however brings the opposite, corrupting the hearts of men bringing distress and despair and wounds that will never heal, grieving the spirit of God.

"She openeth her mouth with wisdom; and in her tongue is the law of kindness." (Proverbs 31:26)

Proverbs 31 is the well-known description of a virtuous woman, one that fears the Lord. When she speaks it is with discretion and prudence. Her gentle words are given for instruction in the wisdom of godly living. With a heart of grace and mercy her kind words are spoken to exhort and edify those in her care.

"By long forbearing is a prince persuaded, and a soft tongue breaketh the bone." (Proverbs 25:15)

Words spoken in anger and arrogance rarely accomplish anything but bitterness and contempt. A patient man how-ever carefully considers not only his words but the timing of his speech. Having patience to wait for the right opportunity to present our thoughts may persuade the hearer to use sound reasoning in contemplating an idea that may be adverse to his beliefs. Harsh words usually meet strong resistance, instinctively protecting the bones from harm. Soft words however, find their way through the thinnest crevices to touch the heart of man, breaking the strong-holds of resistance to bring about peaceful resolutions.

"If any man among you seem to be religious, and bridleth not his tongue, but deceiveth his own heart, this man's religion is vain". (James 1:26)

Probably the most dangerous and certainly unconsecrated use of the tongue is that of the man who seems to be religious, even to the point of believing he is righteous, but then is boastful of his own works. Rather than words of exhortation he inclines to criticize and tear down the character of others. He is the Pharisee, confident that his own works and words will bring about his salvation. The Christian can easily discern his godless character but to the unsaved his enticing words only lead them ever closer to hell. All his religion is useless. Jesus warned us that such men would arise and told us to take heed, (reference Mark 13:22).

In John 14:6 we read "Jesus saith unto him, I am the way, the truth, and the life: no man cometh unto the Father, but by me."

Allow God today to consecrate your tongue to always tell this truth.

XXVII

The Consecrated Ear

"What? know ye not that your body is the temple of the Holy Ghost which is in you, which ye have of God, and ye are not your own? For ye are bought with a price: therefore glorify God in your body, and in your spirit, which are God's". (1 Corinthians 6:19-20)

In the previous chapter we discussed the power we hold in one of our smallest body members, the tongue. We saw how dangerous it can be if left uncontrolled and ruled by our sinful nature. We also saw how profitable it can be for God's kingdom if we allow the Holy Spirit to guide its use. In this chapter we will look at the body member that has the most influence on our mind, our ears.

In the King James Version of the Bible the word ear or ears is used 271 times. I'm pretty sure that means God wants to make sure we listen. Some of those are referring to ears of corn but most relate to hearing. As powerful as our tongue is, our ear is just as essential. Without hearing the tongue has no power.

My wife often tells me that I can't hear, usually when she's trying to tell me something. My hearing is not as acute as it once was due to years of working in noisy environments, however my hearing isn't necessarily the problem. It's the listening that I sometimes have trouble with. Listening to her requires that I focus on what she is saying. If I am reading or listening intently to a television program or simply lost in thought, it can be difficult to instantly shift my focus to what she is saying and I have to ask her to repeat what she just said. Fortunately asking her to re-peat something is not normally a major problem, other than being a bit frustrating for her. But what if she is in trouble and needs my help? What if what she just said is a sensitive matter that she had to muster up the courage to say even once and can't bear to repeat?

Because she is my wife, there should always be at least a small part of my brain that is attentive to her and when a need arises should signal the rest of my being to fully focus on her and call me to action. The same goes for her. That's the best part of a marriage, having contentment in knowing you have one person who will always be there for you.

In the same manner, Christians should always be ready to hear the still small voice of the Holy Spirit. When we fail in our readiness to hear what He says there can be eternal consequences. I know I have failed in that regard many times, but one instance in particular still haunts my memory from time to time. The Spirit once nudged me to call a former coworker that I hadn't seen in a few years. Although I knew he was not a believer, that day I was too busy.

Months went by and the thought of him never entered my mind. When I finally tried to call, he didn't answer. When I began tracking him down, I discovered that he had committed suicide about the same time that I first felt the urge to call him. Maybe I was the one who could have talked him out of that decision, maybe I could have led him to Jesus. I'll never know for sure. I do know I am forgiven, but it was a harsh lesson to show me how crucial it is to keep my ears ready to hear the Holy Spirit's voice. It's a lesson that will stay with me the rest of my life.

> "And let it be, when thou hearest the sound of a going in the tops of the mulberry trees, that then thou shalt bestir thyself: for then shall the LORD go out before thee, to smite the host of the Philistines." (2 Samuel 5:24)

David had just been anointed king of Israel. Almost always when God gives us an opportunity to serve Him we find ourselves under attack. As God's anointed king, David found himself under attack many times during his life. He knew however where to find strength.

God directed David to wait in the mulberry trees and listen. Too many times we get impatient and try to fight the battles by ourselves and that usually ends in failure. If David had not listened as God had instructed him he would have not have succeeded in the fight with the Philistines. No matter how urgent and important we believe a task to be we need to be patient, waiting and listening for God's command to move.

As Christians we need to be careful what we allow our ears to hear. If we constantly listen to the ungodliness and hate that is prevalent in our world, we will become bitter and callous. Our ears should be tuned to always hear the cries for help, knowing that sometimes - most times, those cries are not verbal. We can hear them clearly though through the voice of urging from the Holy Spirit.

Just as we should always have a part of our hearing attentive to our spouse, another part should always be listening for directions from God. We must spend time each day not only in reading and studying God's word but in prayer. The Bible teaches us to "Pray without ceasing" (1Thessalonians 5:17). When we abide in Christ then His voice becomes familiar to us and we can quickly respond when He calls. I can hear my wife's voice across a crowded room because I am familiar with her voice from our daily communication. We must have that same familiarity with the voice of our Savior.

"Bow down thine ear, and hear the words of the wise, and apply thine heart unto my knowledge."(Proverbs 22:17)

"My son, attend to my words; incline thine ear unto my sayings." (Proverbs 4:20)

"Apply thine heart unto instruction, and thine ears to the words of knowledge." (Proverbs 23:12)

"And he read therein before the street that was before the water gate from the morning until midday, before the men and the women, and those that could understand; and the ears of all the people were attentive unto the book of the law." (Nehemiah 8:3)

"What I tell you in darkness, that speak ye in light: and what ye hear in the ear, that preach ye upon the housetops." (Matthew 10:27)

"If any man have an ear, let him hear." (Revelation 13:9)

XXVIII

The Consecrated Eye

"What? know ye not that your body is the temple of the Holy Ghost which is in you, which ye have of God, and ye are not your own? For ye are bought with a price: therefore glorify God in your body, and in your spirit, which are God's." (1 Corinthians 6:19-20)

"The Eye is Not Satisfied" (Ecclesiastes 1:8)

On day three of creation I'm sure God had me on His mind while He gathered the waters and called them the seas. He knew how I would stand in awe at the magnificent sight of the waves constantly crashing on the seashore, at the seemingly infinite expanse of water. He was already planning those glorious colors he would use to paint the heavens when the sun would rise over the Atlantic Ocean bringing with it the promise of a new day. Watching the silent gulls as they effortlessly glide just above the water looking for their next meal makes all the worries and troubles of life fade away into nothingness, if only for a little while.

Every time my wife and I plan a vacation or a short getaway my first choice of destination is always the beach. However, it doesn't matter which way we go there are sights of grandeur in all directions. I don't think anything brings us more physical pleasure than our sight. If God decided to take away all my senses but one I would beg to keep my sight. I'm reminded of Solomon's words in the first chapter of Ecclesiastes, "the eye is not satisfied with seeing". Although I've seen the sunrise thousands of times, I still want to see it again.

As Jesus walked and taught here on earth He used the analogy of sight and blindness many times as a spiritual sense. Although our physical sight seems so important, it is our spiritual sight that allows us to understand the good news of Jesus Christ. In John 9:39 we read "And Jesus said, For judgment I am come into this world, that they which see not might see; and that they which see might be made blind." Jesus had just performed the miracle of giving sight to the man who was blind since birth. As with every miracle He performed, Jesus used it to teach those who were present. First, He had to satisfy the disciples' curiosity as to why the man was blind to begin with. Jesus explained that it isn't necessarily one's sin that causes their misfortunes, rather we are made weak so that God may be glorified by His healing.

Jesus went on to teach the real lesson of the miracle which He directed to the Pharisees in verse 39. Jesus came as Light to expose the darkness of sin and ignorance to those who have a genuine desire for spiritual sight. But to those conceited in their mortal wisdom, thinking themselves to have divine understanding yet lay undue burdens on the common people, these would be blinded and hearts hardened by the true light of Christ. The same S-u-n softens wax and hardens clay. The same S-o-n softens humble hearts and hardens hearts full of pride.

As Christians, we must endure many difficult circumstance and burdens throughout our lives. Although we are never promised physical comfort here in this world, we are instructed where to find strength. In Micah 7:7 we read "Therefore I will look unto the LORD; I will wait for the God of my salvation: my God will hear me." If we are diligent to focus our eyes on Jesus, through reading His word and in prayer, we will find strength to get through each day. When we keep our eyes focused on Jesus our own troubles vanish away, but then we also begin to see not just His face, but what He sees around us. Through Jesus' eyes we see the needs of others around us.

Christ has consecrated each member of the church, His body, for a particular service, and by definition, if Jesus consecrated us then we as individuals are fitted for a specific holy service. Each member of our body then must likewise be consecrated for a specific purpose. In parts 1 and 2 of this series we learned how the tongue and ears complement each other in service to our Lord. When we add con-secration of our eyes to the body, both our physical and spiritual eyes, we begin to better understand how we are fitted together with each member having a specific purpose. It is only with our eyes that we can follow Christ's command; "Lift up your eyes, and look on the fields; for they are white already to harvest."

We must look through Jesus' eyes to see the harvest, listen for the cries out of the darkness, then speak the good news of the gospel of salvation through Jesus Christ.

XXIX

The Consecrated Feet

"What? know ye not that your body is the temple of the Holy Ghost which is in you, which ye have of God, and ye are not your own? For ye are bought with a price: therefore glorify God in your body, and in your spirit, which are God's."
(1 Corinthians 6:19-20)

As the body gets older the aches and pains come more frequently. Since the feet are responsible for carrying the entire weight of the body they tend to cause much suffering if not properly cared for. Doctors tell us that walking even for just a few minutes per day helps keep the blood flowing and our feet flexible therefore less likely to cause us suffering. A good soak in cool water often helps to relieve pain in the feet. The best advice I can think of is wading barefoot in a cold mountain stream. That will bring welcome relief not only to tired *soles* but to tired *souls* as well.

As with the other parts of the body we studied thus far the Bible draws analogies with the physical feet and our spiritual feet. When we walk our feet gather the dust and dirt that's in our path much more than the rest of our body. Many cultures still hold to the tradition of removing one's shoes when entering a home as a sign of respect but there is also the practical reason of keeping as much dirt as possible from entering the home. In much the same way when we as Christians walk about in the world we pick up sin dirt on our spiritual feet.

Jesus said to him, "The one who has bathed does not need to wash, except for his feet, but is completely clean. And you are clean, but not every one of you." (John 13:10 ESV) As Jesus washes His disciples feet, He explains to Peter the continuous gathering of sin-dirt which we collect as we go about our daily life must not be neglected. We need a daily cleansing through repentant prayer. Not only do we need to care for our own feet, but we must keep watch on our fellow Christians with loving humility lest they fall into some dangerous sin. "If I then, your Lord and Teacher, have washed your feet, you also ought to wash one another's feet." (John 13:14 ESV)

"And he said, Draw not nigh hither: put off thy shoes from off thy feet, for the place whereon thou standest is holy ground." (Exodus 3:5)

"And your feet shod with the preparation of the gospel of peace;" (Ephesians 6:15)

"My help cometh from the LORD, which made heaven and earth. He will not suffer thy foot to be moved: he that keepeth thee will not slumber." (Psalms 121:2-3)

"And how shall they preach, except they be sent? as it is written, How beautiful are the feet of them that preach the gospel of peace, and bring glad tidings of good things!" (Romans 10:15)

"He will keep the feet of his saints, and the wicked shall be silent in darkness; for by strength shall no man prevail." (1 Samuel 2:9)

"For thou hast delivered my soul from death: wilt not thou deliver my feet from falling, that I may walk before God in the light of the living?" (Psalms 56:13)

"Teach me thy way, O LORD, and lead me in a plain path, because of mine enemies." (Psalms 27:11)

"Thy word is a lamp unto my feet, and a light unto my path." (Psalms 119:105)

"Ponder the path of thy feet, and let all thy ways be established." (Proverbs 4:26)

XXX

The Consecrated Hands

If the pandemic of 2020 has taught us anything it's how to wash our hands. We have also learned that germs are practically everywhere. As a child of the sixties I spent most of my time outside, in the woods, in the creek, in the dirt. Yes there were roads to build for my toy cars and trucks, holes to dig, frontiers to explore; never a thought or care about getting dirty. I was always reminded though to wash my hands when called inside to supper. If only I had known at the time the story of the Pharisees questioning Jesus about why His disciples ate without washing their hands and Jesus' answer that what enters the body does not defile the body. But then I'm sure my smart mouth would have been swiftly corrected.

Concluding our series on the consecrated body we focus on how to prepare our hands for serving God. Keeping our hands free of dirt and grime may be a healthy habit, but it certainly isn't necessary in order to please our Lord. Each of us has a distinct calling. For some it may well be to have dirt free hands while caring for the sick or preparing food. Others are called to work the fields and farms, getting dirty in the process, to produce food. Both jobs are equally important, both allow opportunity to honor God, yet they are at opposite ends of the cleanliness spectrum.

How then do we prepare our hands for service? It is likely that King David wrote the 24th Psalm as he led men to retrieve the stolen ark of the covenant and carry it to its rightful place in Jerusalem. Verse four describes what is required for such a privileged task. Our hands must not be soiled with sinful acts thereby defiling even to the heart. Our hands must be guarded from reaching after vain affections and worldly treasures which can never satisfy our soul.

"Who shall ascend into the hill of the LORD? or who shall stand in his holy place? He that hath clean hands, and a pure heart; who hath not lifted up his soul unto vanity, nor sworn deceitfully." (Psalms 24:3-4)

James put it rather bluntly to the hypocritical leaders of the church who outwardly make a show of righteousness yet still walk hand in hand with the sinful world. Our hands must put away the worldly lusts, be separated completely from sin with a repentant heart in order to enjoy a holy communion with God in worship.

"Draw nigh to God, and he will draw nigh to you. Cleanse your hands, ye sinners; and purify your hearts, ye double minded." (James 4:8)

Honoring God with our hands is more than just maintaining godly cleanliness. We must train our hands to be competent and skillful in whatever task is given us. Whether our job is flipping burgers or building rocket ships, we can honor God by continually striving to do our very best at our job.

"Whatsoever thy hand findeth to do, do it with thy might; for there is no work, nor device, nor knowledge, nor wisdom, in the grave, whither thou goest." (Ecclesiastes 9:10)

"And that ye study to be quiet, and to do your own business, and to work with your own hands, as we commanded you;" (1

Thessalonians 4:11)

There is no greater honor to God than lifting up hands in praise, prayer, and worship; hands that signify a heart softened and purified with the blood of Jesus Christ. All our labor is in vain if we fail to reach up first calling on the one true holy God. Only by first reaching up can we reach out as holy instruments in the hand of our Savior.

"I will therefore that men pray every where, lifting up holy hands, without wrath and doubting." (1 Timothy 2:8)

"And by the hands of the apostles were many signs and wonders wrought among the people; (and they were all with one accord in Solomon's porch." (Acts 5:12)

Our body is made of many parts and each part is vital to the whole. Neglecting a splinter in the toe could eventually disable the whole body if it becomes infected and untreated. We must be diligent in quickly removing the things which can debilitate us. The church is also a body of many parts and each part is equally vital. More importantly, each part is loved and cared for equally by the head of the church, Jesus Christ. In the same way the tiny splinter can disable our body, a seemingly insignificant hidden sin in one member can hinder the ministry of the whole church. We honor God by keeping a watchful eye on ourselves, rooting out and discarding those sin splinters, disallowing even the slightest appearance of ungodliness. We need each other to keep us accountable before our Father.

"But exhort one another daily, while it is called To day; lest any of you be hardened through the deceitfulness of sin." (Hebrews 3:13)

"For as the body is one, and hath many members, and all the members of that one body, being many, are one body: so also is Christ. For by one Spirit are we all baptized into one body, whether we be Jews or Gentiles, whether we be bond or free; and have been all made to drink into one Spirit. For the body is not one member, but many." (1 Corinthians 12:12-14)

XXXI

Baptism

"For by one Spirit are we all baptized into one body, whether we be Jews or Gentiles, whether we be bond or free; and have been all made to drink into one Spirit. (1 Corinthians 12:13)

From the moment we believe in our heart and confess with our mouth that the resurrected Christ Jesus is Lord we are immediately immersed in His body. Spiritual baptism simply means our soul has experienced the same death, burial, and resurrection as Jesus did bodily, whereby He makes us a part of His body. By submitting to the ordinance of water baptism, a believer testifies that God has performed this spiritual baptism in him.

I am grateful this morning that nothing in this world or beyond this world can separate me from the body of Christ, not because of anything I do or say, but by the power of God, which is greater than all.

XXXII

Break the Perfume Jar

"But when his disciples saw it, they had indignation, saying, To what purpose is this waste?"
(Matthew 26:8)

My favorite comedian of all time is Jerry Clower. He often spun outlandish tales revolving around his fictitious family, the Ledbetters and the predicaments they got into. As if the stories weren't enough to draw you in, his southern Mississippi accent and snorting laugh could keep you laughing 'til it hurt. Jerry would find ways to weave in his Christian upbringing in many of his stories, making them relatable to anyone in his audience.

I recall one story in particular about Uncle Versie Ledbetter, who happened to be the oldest deacon in the church. He didn't attend many of their meetings though. He preferred to let the younger men, those in their 50's and 60's take care of the church business. But Uncle Versie heard that the deacons were going to vote on spending some money, so he made sure he was at that meeting. The deacons were voting to buy a chandelier. Uncle Versie spoke up in protest. "Nobody in church has enough education to spell it on the Sears order form. If they got it nobody in church knew how to play it. We shouldn't spend money on a chandelier as bad as we need lights in the church." I guess we can say Uncle Versie was a practical man and saw no need for extravagances.

Websters Dictionary defines extravagance this way.

• a going beyond reasonable or proper limits in conduct or speech; unreasonable excess

• a spending of more than is reasonable or necessary; excessive expenditure; wastefulness

• an instance of excess in spending, behavior, or speech

I recall the church budget discussions we had around the time of the 2010 recession and how some things were seen as necessary by some but seen as not as important to others. I think that time was good for us as a church because it gave us an opportunity to reaffirm God's will for each of us individually. We had to ask, is the ministry path I'm on really God's will or is it what I want to do? Sometimes we get our mind set as to what the church ought to be doing without really asking the One in charge. Jesus Christ is still our chief cornerstone.

We find an example of extravagance that Jesus approved of in Matthew 26:6-13.

Verse 6 begins, "Now when Jesus was in Bethany, in the house of Simon the leper," Bethany is about two miles east of Jerusalem near the Mount of Olives. It is where Jesus resided his last few weeks before His crucifixion. This Simon is believed to the one of the ten Jesus healed that returned to thank him. Note he is still called "the leper". Even though our sins are forgiven, the world's view of our past deeds doesn't necessarily change. Jesus' blood paid the price for our eternal soul, not this corruptible body. The parallel story in John 12 tells us that Lazarus, whom Jesus had raised from the dead, sat at the table and that Martha, Lazarus' sister, was serving supper, and Mary, the other sister, is the one we read about in verse 7. This takes place just before the last supper with the disciples. So, this was sort of a last supper with those that were closest friends, those outside the circle of disciples who knew Jesus not only as their savior but as a human friend.

In verse 7 we read, "There came unto him a woman having an alabaster box of very precious ointment, and poured it on his head, as he sat at meat." As the gospels of John and Mark relate this same event, they describe the ointment as a pound of spikenard and its worth about a year's wages at that time. It's still used by some practicing herbal and natural healers, but the cost is significantly lower. It's in the same family as the Valerian plant which is a more widely known herbal remedy. The oil or ointment is made from the roots of the spikenard plant. It has several medicinal properties but the one I found most interesting is that it is used in palliative care to help ease the transition from life to death. Remember Jesus told in verse 2 that He is about to be crucified. So Mary here is wasting no time. She even interrupts the men at mealtime. Do we sometimes hold back our worship, our praise, for a more convenient time? Can we even know what we may have missed by doing so?

In verses 8-9 we see the Uncle Versie attitude come out in the disciples. "But when his disciples saw it, they had indignation, saying, To what purpose is this waste? For this ointment might have been sold for much, and given to the poor."

Indignation here means contempt, disgust, even angry. John names Judas as the one who voices this indignation, but Mark infers that it was not just Judas, but others had indignation "within themselves". The reference here is to one of the Jewish laws given by Moses in Deuteronomy chapter 15 that the poor should be taken care of by those that had the means to do it. Just back one chapter Jesus had told them they were to feed the hungry, clothe the na-ked, and visit the sick and imprisoned. So maybe to them in their misunderstanding of the intents of her heart, it seemed she was doing the opposite of what Jesus had just told them.

Verse 10 says "When Jesus understood it, he said unto them, Why trouble ye the woman? for she hath wrought a good work upon me." Aren't you glad Jesus understands? Commentaries interpret this as Jesus understanding the men's indignation, but He also understood Mary's desire to show her love for her savior, to worship and praise Him. If it had been Pharisees speaking against her, I don't think she would have been troubled in the least, but this was Jesus' disciples, the ones closest to Him who should have understood her worship. Imagine how she must have felt when they became angry at her for worshiping with her whole heart the One they call Lord. Jesus goes on to say she had done a "good work". It was done to honor and glorify Him and it came from a real and sincere love.

In verse 11, Jesus continues "For ye have the poor always with you; but me ye have not always." referring to the earthly physical body, for we know that Jesus said he would never leave us or forsake us. Sometimes we are so intent on sticking to the plan that we miss out on the great opportunities. We need to be sensitive to the leading of the Holy Spirit. Many opportunities to serve have been passed over because they didn't fit our plan and many of those will never be presented to us again.

Jesus explains in verses 12-13 "For in that she hath poured this ointment on my body, she did it for my burial. Verily I say unto you, Wheresoever this gospel shall be preached in the whole world, there shall also this, that this woman hath done, be told for a memorial of her."

I don't think that Mary fully understood what she had done. She was obedient to the Holy Spirit in love and worship for the Messiah, but she didn't realize that she was as Jesus said, preparing His body for burial. She certainly didn't think that this event would be recorded and handed down through the ages to instruct us to be extravagant in worship. God's will is accomplished through our obedience. God's plans and intentions are not always fully revealed to us when He asks us to do something. Think about the impact this had on Mary's life. The transition from being hurt and broken by the opinions of men, to the joy and peace she must felt from the words of Christ, that this simple act of obedience would be told for a memorial of her whenever the gospel was preached throughout the whole world.

Our lesson in these verses is to "break the perfume jar" for Jesus. These seven verses tell the story of one woman's act of worship, seen by some as extravagant, but ordained by Christ himself to be told throughout the generations as a memorial of her. We cannot know how many lives have been changed from hearing or reading this story. How many lives will be changed if you step out on faith, in simple obedience to the Holy Spirit, and show your love for Jesus in ways the world doesn't understand?

XXXIII

Be Ready

"But sanctify the Lord God in your hearts: and be ready always to give an answer to every man that asketh you a reason of the hope that is in you with meekness and fear:"
(1 Peter 3:15)

Whether you admit it or not, we all crave attention. We want people to hear what we have to say. Our world has driven many of us to sharing frivolous nonsense on social media, then agonizing over how many likes and follows we get. Going "viral" is now the ultimate excitement.

Truth is that people are watching us wherever we go. If we claim to be a follower of Christ, we are watched even closer. God calls us to be a peculiar people. Why would He do that you ask? So that people might take notice of our gratitude and praise toward God. (ref. 1 Peter 2:9).

When we attract attention for God's glory, it awakens a curiosity in those around us. As Peter tells us in our focus verse, we must be ready to answer questions about our faith. When talking about our faith, we need to be honest. We should not try to hide our flaws or pretend that we are perfect. We need to be open about our own journey and allow others to see that we are real people who have struggles just like them.

How can we prepare ourselves for the questions? Spending time each day reading God's word and in prayer is vital to our readiness. The most effective message you can give someone is to tell them how you came to trust in Christ. That is your witness that no one can dispute. But as the apostle Paul warns young Timothy, (ref. 2 Tim. 2:23) we must avoid getting side-tracked into foolish questions which will certainly lead to arguments and do nothing to further God's kingdom. Always allow the Holy Spirit to guide your answers. Allowing God to continuously transform your life through His word and in prayer will prepare you to not only be ready, but confidently await any questions about the hope within you.

XXXIV

A Determined Choice

"Woe is me!" The prophet Micah laments his circumstances in the seventh chapter of his discourse to the leaders of Israel, speaking of the wickedness surrounding him. We can sympathize with Micah's plight today. Our leaders seem to have no regard for the people. In chapter 2, Micah describes those in power as devising evil at night to practice when the morning light comes. Their greed drove them to oppress the common people without any sign of remorse. Judges required bribes for their verdicts. The rich and powerful would entangle their mischief in the courts allowing them to continue their evil ways. Sound familiar?

Micah was given the unpopular task of proclaiming God's impending judgement on Israel. His bold witness for God was believed by a few and rejected by many. In chapter 7 Micah speaks of discord within close family members. The controversies caused by his witness surely affected his mental state. We can easily be discouraged at the mockery of God we see around us.

But Micah made a determined choice to trust God. In verses 7-8

we read; "Therefore I will look unto the LORD; I will wait for the God of my salvation: my God will hear me. Rejoice not against me, O mine enemy: when I fall, I shall arise; when I sit in darkness, the LORD shall be a light unto me."
(Micah 7:7-8)
We can easily get distressed if we watch all the evil going on around us. It may seem like the whole world is against us. But like Micah, we must determine to look unto the LORD, trust Him, and allow Him to be our light in this dark world. God gives rest to the weary, strength to the down-trodden, and comfort to the brokenhearted.

XXXV

Spiritual Growth

Our spiritual growth is dependent on three distinct intentional relationships. The first is our relationship with God which requires daily nurturing. The second is with someone who we look to as a mentor and serves not only as an advisor or a teacher, but as an accountability partner. The third is with believers who tend to shy away from getting involved in the ministry of the church. These may be new converts just finding their way, or it could be older Christians who have allowed the cares of this world to distract them from their divine purpose. Either of those will challenge us to grow in our own faith, to study to be approved as an acceptable servant in God's eyes. When we are diligent to maintain those three relationships, our primary task of reaching the lost with the gospel of Christ becomes much less intimidating.

"Study to shew thyself approved unto God, a workman that needeth not to be ashamed, rightly dividing the word of truth." (2 Timothy 2:15)

XXXVI

Christians and Controversy

"Keep yourselves in the love of God, looking for the mercy of our Lord Jesus Christ unto eternal life. And of some have compassion, making a difference: And others save with fear, pulling them out of the fire; hating even the garment spotted by the flesh." (Jude 1:21-23)

A transition occurred in our world in the late 70's to early 80's when we moved from the industrial age to the information age. There was a time not so long ago that if you wanted your opinion heard you could write a letter to the editor of your local newspaper. If your letter was deemed appropriate for readers, (yes, editors once had a moral conscience) it would be edited simply for grammar, spelling, and punctuation and printed. The opinion then would be the topic of the day at the breakfast and lunch cafes. Maybe something would be accomplished to make the community a better place to live or maybe the idea would be dropped in favor of the one in the next day's letter to the editor.

The explosion of the internet changed all that. Virtually eliminating restrictions to communication has given every person the ability to project their opinion to a global audience within a fraction of a second. What a remarkable concept. What great things we can now accomplish. Except for this, "The heart is deceitful above all things, and desperately wicked: who can know it?" (Jeremiah 17:9)

Turn on your television or access the internet and you'll likely be bombarded with controversial opinions. Opinions that, because our heart is naturally evil, are inclined to promote division. Division then brings destruction and de-cay. This rapid decay has brought on anxieties, hopelessness, and depression at a staggering rate. We see Christians, even some deeply rooted in their faith, fall into the snares of the division that is being loudly proclaimed. We live in an "I am right, you are wrong" world and so we respond by claiming our God given rights cannot be taken away.

God given rights? Can we make a list? Sorry, it's not technically a list when we only have two. We have the right to accept Jesus Christ as our Lord and Savior. And number two, we have the right to reject Jesus Christ as our Lord and Savior. Anything else we have is through God's grace and mercy and therefore subject to His sovereignty. When we fully surrender to Christ and accept this fact then we can enjoy the peace from God instead of suffering the anxieties of the world.

So, you ask, does this mean Christians must refrain from involvement in the world's controversies? Do we not take a stand against what we know to be wrong? Absolutely we need to take a stand. However, we must be careful to keep our emotions and feelings, not to mention our language, in check. Our activities against injustices of the world must be prompted and guided by the Holy Spirit and our position must be in line with God's word. Our priorities must follow the words that Jesus gave His disciples, "Then shall they also answer him, saying, Lord, when saw we thee an hungred, or athirst, or a stranger, or naked, or sick, or in prison, and did not minister unto thee? Then shall he answer them, saying, Verily I say unto you, Inasmuch as ye did it not to one of the least of these, ye did it not to me." (Matthew 25:44-45)

Jesus allowed His anger to be known when He overturned the tables of the money changers in the temple. Imagine arriving at your church for Sunday morning worship and finding someone sitting at the entrance charging an admission fee. Would you follow Christ's example by stopping such an ungodly activity? I know that is an unlikely scenario, but consider carefully, are there activities going on in your church that are disrespectful or irreverent toward God? I pray not, but as the body of Christ we must keep a watchful eye on ourselves to ensure we are in God's will before we can challenge the injustices in the world. In Jesus' words, "Ye are the salt of the earth: but if the salt have lost his savour, wherewith shall it be salted? it is thenceforth good for nothing, but to be cast out, and to be trodden under foot of men." (Matthew 5:13)

We can face the world's controversies if we meet them with compassion, driven by the Holy Spirit within us. Our first priority however is always to teach the gospel of salvation through Jesus Christ. Each soul we win for Christ is one that is not against us. For if we are together with Christ, we should be in harmony with each other.

XXXVII

Do You Love Much?

"Wherefore I say unto thee, Her sins, which are many, are forgiven; for she loved much: but to whom little is forgiven, the same loveth little". (Luke 7:47)

Do you love much or do you love little? The power of Christ's church can only be manifested through Christians who love much. Does that mean God only uses people who had the greater sin? Of course not.

God uses people who never forget that without His forgiveness that they were dead in sin without any hope. Without the zealous love that we owe our Savior we become nothing more than dry bones in the valley. Only through faith was Ezekiel able to see life in the valley full of dry bones.

Christians, be mindful to always love much. Much love brings much life...eternal life.

"Father, today I thank you for the much love you showed me through your Son Jesus Christ. It was your love that put flesh upon my dry bones and brought the four winds to breathe life into me. Lord I realize that my sin, whether great or small, is enough to separate me from You. But You restored my life with the blood sacrifice of Jesus. Father use my life to show much love to all I meet. In Jesus name, and for His sake I pray. Amen."

XXXVIII

Father, If It Pleases You

"When the king held out the golden scepter to Esther, Esther rose and stood before the king. And she said, "If it please the king, and if I have found favor in his sight, and if the thing seems right before the king, and I am pleasing in his eyes, let an order be written to revoke the letters de-vised by Haman the Agagite, the son of Hammedatha, which he wrote to destroy the Jews who are in all the provinces of the king." (Esther 8:4-5)

When queen Esther comes before her earthly king to plea for the lives of her kindred she bows with reverence and humbly offers her submission to his will. Shouldn't we offer the same and more so to our heavenly Father when we fall before Him in prayer?

Father, if it pleases You to grant my desires.
Father, if I am favored in your sight through the shed blood of your Son.
Father, if my request is according to your divine will.
Father, if I am pleasing in your eyes.

Our heavenly Father is the King of kings, Lord of lords, who created and sustains all the universe. Yet we are His prize, the crown of His creation. It is our Father's desire to have intimate fellowship with us. What a hum-bling thought. The God of all creation wants to sit with you and me and hear what's on our heart.

XXXIX

A Morning Prayer

*Kind and gracious heavenly Father, what an honor and privilege it is
to kneel at your feet in prayer.*
*You are the omniscient, omnipresent, omnipotent, sovereign, holy God of
all that exists.*
I know You are busy feeding the sparrows.
*You are pushing the tender leaves from the thin branches as they sway
from the cool morning breeze you blow upon them.*
*You are unfolding the delicate petals of the flowers, directing the bees into
their nectar, then guiding their flight back to the hive to create the sweet
honey that we can enjoy*
*You are averting the eyes of the fox so that the young rabbit can enjoy
nibbling tender leaves of clover throughout the day*
*You chose the incredible colors to paint the sky this morning and have
already planned each minute detail of the Your daily masterpiece we often
simply call sunset.*
*You arrange each fluffy cloud in magnificent arrays that catch our eye,
inspiring us to compare each one's shape to perhaps some animal floating*

across the sky.
You hold each raindrop until it's just the right time for it to fall, in just the
right place, so it may soften the hard shell of the tiny seed, breaking it
open sprouting forth a new life from lifelessness.
All this and so much more than I can fathom,
You still take time to hear my prayer,
often whispering back in that familiar still small voice.
What an Awesome God you are!
Amen.

XL

God Loves You

There is Hope. There is a power capable of giving us hope and the ability to change our direction in life.

Romans 1:16 "For I am not ashamed of the gospel of Christ: for it is the power of God unto salvation to every one that believeth; to the Jew first, and also to the Greek."

What is the problem? We cannot live a perfect life no matter how hard we try. God is holy, meaning He cannot be associated with even the tiniest wrong thing that we do.

Romans 3:23 "For all have sinned, and come short of the glory of God;"

What is the consequence? The punishment for even the smallest of sin is death. Death in this context not only means a physical death but also an eternal separation from God. Though the consequence of our sin is harshly pointed out, God is merciful to provide His solution in the same verse.

Romans 6:23 "For the wages of sin is death; but the gift of God is eternal life through Jesus Christ our Lord."

What did God do for us? When Jesus, who came in the form of a man and lived a sinless life here on earth, and gave His life on the cross He took our punishment for us. He conquered death when He arose on the third day. By taking our punishment He made a way for us to be reconciled to God the Father.

Romans 5:8 "But God commendeth his love toward us, in that, while we were yet sinners, Christ died for us."

How does God want us to respond? Although God made the way for us to be saved, to be called His people, we must accept His gift. We must believe in what He has done for us and we must proclaim it before men.

Romans 10:9-10 "That if thou shalt confess with thy mouth the Lord Jesus, and shalt believe in thine heart that God hath raised him from the dead, thou shalt be saved. For with the heart man believeth unto righteousness; and with the mouth confession is made unto salvation."
Romans 10:13 "For whosoever shall call upon the name of the Lord shall be saved."

Trust God's word that the death of Christ paid for our sin, believe that God raised him physically from death to life, and confess your faith and trust in Him. Trust means Repent, turning away from sin and following God's direction. Believe means Accepting

God's word as absolute Truth. Confess means acknowledging Jesus Christ as the supreme authority over your life.

What is the Result? The most precious promises ever made!

Romans 5:1 "Therefore being justified by faith, we have peace with God through our Lord Jesus Christ:"

Romans 8:1 "There is therefore now no condemnation to them which are in Christ Jesus, who walk not after the flesh, but after the Spirit."

Romans 8:38-39 "For I am persuaded, that neither death, nor life, nor angels, nor principalities, nor powers, nor things present, nor things to come, Nor height, nor depth, nor any other creature, shall be able to separate us from the love of God, which is in Christ Jesus our Lord."

If you are ready to accept God's promises for your life, you can today. This simple prayer can be the start of a brand new life in Christ Jesus. You can say it in your own words if you want. God knows the intent of your heart and He will hear you.

Dear God, I am a sinner and need your forgiveness. I believe that Jesus Christ died for my sin and is raised from death to life. I am willing to turn from my sin and follow you. Jesus I ask you to come in my heart, save me and lead my life. Thank you for saving me. Amen.

If you have prayed this prayer and accepted God's gift of salvation through Jesus Christ, the next step is to find a local Bible believing church and tell the pastor that you have accepted Jesus Christ. In the meantime you should begin reading at least a few verses of the Bible every day. A good place to start is the New Testament book of John. Spend time every day in prayer. It doesn't require any special words, just tell God what's on your mind and ask Him to help you live your life for Him. The Bible says that you are now a new creature and the Holy Spirit resides in you to guide you every minute.

"Therefore if any man be in Christ, he is a new creature: old things are passed away; behold, all things are become new." (2 Corinthians 5:17)